Douro Valley Travel Guide 2025

DOURO VALLEY TRAVEL GUIDE 2025

Exploring the Natural Wonders, Outdoor Adventures, and Delectable Cuisine of Northern Portugal's Jewel.

BY

RONALD T. MILLER

Douro Valley Travel Guide 2025

All right reserved. No part of this publication should be reproduced, distributed, or transmitted in any form or by any means, including photocopying, recording, or other electronic or mechanical methods, without the prior written permission of the publisher, except in the case of brief quotations embodied in critical reviews and certain other noncommercial uses permitted by copyright law.

Copyright@ Ronald T. Miller, 2025.

Douro Valley Travel Guide 2025

Table of Contents

Chapter 1
  Introduction to Douro Valley: Essential Information to Know
  Topography, Borders, and Population in Douro Valley
Chapter 2
  How to Get to Douro Valley
Chapter 3
  Ideal Seasons Tourists Should Visit Douro Valley
  Festivals and Events in Douro Valley
Chapter 4
  Accommodation Options for Tourists in Douro Valley: Top 10 Hotels to Stay
  Transportation Options within Douro Valley: Routes, Prices, and Real-Life Examples
Chapter 5
  Beaches in Douro Valley for Tourists to Explore
  Historical Sites and Monuments in Douro Valley
  Outdoor Activities for Tourists to Explore in Douro Valley
Chapter 6
  Top Foods for Tourists in Douro Valley (and Their Health Benefits)
  Top Restaurants to Visit in Douro Valley with Their Signature Dishes
Chapter 7
  Local Crafts and Souvenirs in Douro Valley for Tourists
  Popular Shopping Centers in Douro Valley

Douro Valley Travel Guide 2025

Chapter 8

    Nightlife Activities for Tourists to Explore in Douro Valley

    7 Days Itinerary Plans for Tourists in Douro Valley

Chapter 1

Introduction to Douro Valley: Essential Information to Know

Tucked into the northern heart of Portugal, the Douro Valley is a living postcard of rolling vineyards, shimmering river bends, and villages where time seems to take a coffee break. Often called the enchanted valley (Vale Encantado), this region is not just a pretty face; it's a UNESCO World Heritage Site, a wine lover's dream, and a slice of Portugal that feels almost untouched by the frantic pace of modern life.

Where Exactly Is the Douro Valley?

The Douro Valley stretches from the Spanish border to the city of Porto, following the meandering Douro River. It covers several sub-regions but is most famous for the Upper Douro (Alto Douro) — the birthplace of Port wine. The valley is a couple of hours' drive from Porto, making it an irresistible getaway for city explorers looking to swap concrete for vineyards.

Why Is the Douro Valley So Special?

Douro Valley Travel Guide 2025

Besides being achingly beautiful, the Douro Valley is the oldest demarcated wine region in the world, officially established in 1756. That's right — the French were still figuring things out when the Portuguese were busy building stone walls to carve their vineyards into the hills.

The valley's steep terraced hillsides aren't just scenic; they are a masterclass in agricultural engineering. And the river itself? It's not just a lazy ribbon of water—it once served as the main highway for rabelos, flat-bottomed boats that transported barrels of precious Port wine downstream to Porto.

Whether you're here for the world-class wines, the river cruises, or the sheer, heart-clutching beauty of the landscape, the Douro Valley delivers a kind of magic that's hard to bottle (although, spoiler alert: they try with the wine).

Essential Things to Know Before You Go

Getting There: Most travelers arrive via Porto. From there, you can rent a car (recommended for flexibility), take a scenic train ride, or book a river cruise.

Douro Valley Travel Guide 2025

Best Time to Visit: Spring (April–June) and fall (September–October) are dreamy, with mild weather and vineyard colors ranging from lush green to fiery gold.

Currency: Euro (€)

Language: Portuguese is spoken, but you'll find that many in the tourism industry know English, especially around wine estates.

Climate: Hot, dry summers and mild, rainy winters. Pack sunscreen if you're visiting between May and September!

Now, to spice things up for your journey, let's share 20 funny and surprising facts about the Douro Valley you won't find in your average guidebook.

20 Funny and Fascinating Facts About Douro Valley

1. Port Wine Was Born Out of an Argument. British merchants added brandy to wine to "stabilize" it during shipping — the wine didn't need help, but they wanted stronger drinks!

2. The Terraces Could Wrap Around the Earth. If you lined up all the vineyard walls built by hand, they could

circle the planet — or at least, it would feel like it after one too many glasses of Port.

3. There's a Train Just for Gawking. The Douro Line train was basically invented for people who like to lean out of windows and say "Wow" every two minutes.

4. You Might See More Sheep Than People. Especially in the smaller villages where sheep are treated like honorary citizens.

5. Locals Compete for "Best Grape Stomper." Yes, foot-stomping grapes is still a thing here — and no, socks are not allowed.

6. There's a Vineyard That Looks Like a Maze from the Air. Quinta do Crasto's aerial view looks like a puzzle you'd need wine to solve.

7. The River Once Had "Pirates." Well, wine pirates — locals who tried to steal barrels off boats as they floated downstream.

8. The Valley Has Its Own Mythology. Some locals swear that singing to the vines helps the grapes grow faster (wine-lullabies, if you will).

9. The Word "Douro" Means "Golden." Probably because the valley shines like treasure at sunset.

10. Vineyard Dogs Are Treated Like Royalty. At some quintas (estates), the dog has a better house than the winemaker.

11. Tourists Often Mistake Vineyards for Art Installations. Seriously, those perfect terraces and vine rows look way too good to be "natural."

12. The Bridges Are Instagram Legends. Especially the one Gustave Eiffel (yes, that Eiffel) designed near Peso da Régua.

13. Locals Believe Their Olive Oil Is Liquid Gold. And they're not wrong — tasting olive oil here could ruin supermarket brands forever.

14. Every Quinta Has a Crazy Story. Including haunted barrels, forbidden love, and runaway goats.

15. It's Totally Normal to Have Wine at Breakfast. Especially during the harvest festival. Don't fight it.

16. Port Tasting Might "Accidentally" Take All Day. It starts as one sip... and ends as a lifestyle.

17. There's a Dish Called "Drunken Rabbit." And no, it's not because the rabbit had too much Port.

18. Pigeons Were Once Used for Wine Messages. Forget texting — pigeons were the original "grapevine" news.

19. The Douro River Changes Color. Depending on the season and light, it can look blue, green, silver, or like molten gold.

20. People Still Debate Which Side of the River is Better. Even if both sides are basically paradise, friendly rivalry is alive and well.

Other Important Things Tourists Should Know

Wine Tourism Is King: You can tour multiple quintas in a day, learning about everything from ancient grape varieties to modern techniques (and tasting plenty along the way).

River Cruises Are Worth It: Whether you opt for a two-hour cruise or a multi-day voyage, floating down the Douro offers some of the most unforgettable views imaginable.

Stay Overnight if You Can: While it's tempting to do a day trip from Porto, staying overnight at a vineyard or a charming village like Pinhão lets you soak up the magic once the tour buses leave.

The Food Is as Good as the Wine: Think roasted lamb, river fish, and desserts dripping with honey and almonds.

Topography, Borders, and Population in Douro Valley

A Landscape Carved by Time

The Douro Valley's topography is a spectacular symphony of steep slopes, winding valleys, and rugged cliffs. Here, the land is anything but flat; it rises and falls in dramatic fashion, sculpted by ancient geological shifts and the tireless work of the Douro River, which has carved deep gorges and rolling hills through layers of schist and granite. This undulating terrain is both a blessing and a challenge—it demands creativity from its people and rewards them with landscapes of jaw-dropping splendor.

The valley's iconic terraced vineyards, a UNESCO World Heritage Site, cling precariously to the hillsides. These man-made marvels, painstakingly built stone by stone over centuries, are a testament to human resilience and ingenuity. Without these terraces, the cultivation of vines would be near impossible in the steep terrain. Walking among them, one feels the pulse of generations who have shaped the land with their hands.

At lower elevations, near the riverbanks, olive groves and almond orchards spread out, their silvery leaves catching the golden Portuguese sunlight. Higher up, the slopes become wilder, cloaked in Mediterranean scrub and dotted with cork oaks and pine forests. Every turn of the road or trail in the Douro Valley offers a new vantage point—a different arrangement of light, land, and water that feels almost otherworldly.

Defining the Borders of the Douro Valley

While there is no rigid political boundary that defines the Douro Valley, its heart undeniably follows the course of the Douro River, from the city of Peso da Régua upstream to the Spanish border. Geographically, the valley is often considered to begin around Mesão Frio, where the river carves its way into the mountainous terrain, and it extends eastward toward towns like Pinhão, São João da Pesqueira, and Vila Nova de Foz Côa.

The Douro River itself acts as a lifeline, threading together the various landscapes, towns, and villages into a cohesive whole. It also serves as a historical boundary between different cultural and economic regions within Portugal. To the north, the valley climbs toward the highlands of Trás-os-Montes, a rugged and more isolated area, while to the south, it merges gradually into the Beira Interior, known for its undulating hills and sleepy towns.

Bordering Spain to the east, the Douro becomes a natural frontier. Here, the river narrows into the stunning Arribes del Duero canyons, where towering cliffs rise sharply from the water's edge, creating a dramatic backdrop unlike anywhere else in the valley. This borderland is less touched by tourism and retains a raw, untouched quality that adventurous travelers find especially captivating.

A Tapestry of Small Communities

Population in the Douro Valley is sparse compared to Portugal's urban centers. Scattered across the hills are small towns and villages where time seems to slow down. Communities like Lamego, Peso da Régua, and Pinhão serve as local hubs, but even they maintain a cozy, small-town charm rather than the hustle and bustle of city life.

Most villages in the valley have populations in the hundreds rather than thousands. Traditional stone houses, whitewashed churches, and cobbled streets are the norm, with life revolving around agriculture, particularly viticulture. The famed Port wine industry, deeply intertwined with the valley's identity, sustains many of these communities, providing livelihoods that have persisted for generations.

Interestingly, the population of the Douro Valley has seen a slow but steady decline over the past century. Many young people have migrated to larger cities like Porto or Lisbon in search of work, leaving behind aging communities. However, recent interest in wine tourism and rural getaways has sparked a gentle revival. Boutique hotels, restored quintas (wine estates), and gourmet restaurants are breathing new life into the valley, attracting visitors who crave authenticity and tranquility.

A Land of Diversity

Though the Douro Valley might seem like a singular entity, its topography and microclimates create a patchwork of distinct subregions, each with its own character. The western part of the valley, closer to Porto, is lusher and greener, benefiting from the Atlantic influence. Rainfall is more abundant here, nurturing not only vineyards but also orchards, fields, and gardens.

Douro Valley Travel Guide 2025

As one moves eastward, the climate becomes drier and more extreme, with hotter summers and colder winters. The soils, too, shift subtly—richer in granite in the west, increasingly schistose toward the heart of the valley. These variations have a profound impact on viticulture, influencing the types of grapes grown and the styles of wine produced.

This geographic diversity ensures that no two areas of the Douro Valley feel exactly alike. A drive from Peso da Régua to Foz Côa is not just a journey through space, but a passage through different worlds—each with its own sights, scents, and sounds.

Chapter 2

How to Get to Douro Valley

Visiting the Douro Valley is a dream for many travelers eager to explore its terraced vineyards, charming villages, and serene river landscapes. Getting there can be an adventure in itself, and depending on your starting point and preferences, there are several convenient ways to reach this stunning region.

By Air: Nearest Airports

Flying into Portugal is the fastest way to begin your Douro Valley journey. While the valley itself does not have a commercial airport, several nearby options make it easily accessible.

1. Francisco Sá Carneiro Airport (Porto Airport)

The closest major airport to the Douro Valley is Francisco Sá Carneiro Airport, located in Porto. It is about 120 kilometers (75 miles) from Peso da Régua, one of the main towns in the Douro. The airport handles numerous international and domestic flights daily, making it a convenient gateway for travelers from Europe and beyond.

2. Lisbon Humberto Delgado Airport

Although further away, Lisbon's Humberto Delgado Airport is another option. It is roughly 360 kilometers (about 220 miles) south of the Douro Valley. If you plan to explore Portugal a bit more extensively, starting in Lisbon and working your way up can be a rewarding experience.

3. Vigo-Peinador Airport (Spain)

For those coming from Spain, Vigo Airport is a lesser-known but viable alternative. Located about 200 kilometers (125 miles) from the Douro Valley, it offers another entry point, especially for travelers combining Northern Spain with Northern Portugal.

4. Tips for Air Travelers

Book flights that arrive early in the day if you intend to continue your journey to the valley the same day.

Consider renting a car directly from the airport if you prefer the freedom of driving through the picturesque countryside.

Check seasonal flight options, as summer months often bring additional routes into Porto from European cities.

By Train: Routes and Timetables

Traveling to the Douro Valley by train is one of the most scenic options, offering stunning views as you glide alongside the Douro River.

5. Porto's São Bento and Campanhã Stations

Most journeys to the Douro Valley by train start at Porto's São Bento or Campanhã train stations. São Bento, famous for its magnificent azulejo tilework, provides a beautiful start to your adventure, while Campanhã offers a larger selection of long-distance trains.

6. Linha do Douro (Douro Line)

The Linha do Douro is the rail line that connects Porto to the heart of the valley. It's a legendary journey, where trains meander through the countryside, hugging the curves of the river and offering postcard-perfect views at every turn.

7. Popular Train Destinations in the Valley

Douro Valley Travel Guide 2025

Peso da Régua: The gateway to wine country and river cruises.

Pinhão: A charming village surrounded by some of the region's most famous vineyards.

Tua: A more remote destination offering breathtaking scenery for the adventurous traveler.

8. Timetable Essentials

Trains from Porto to Peso da Régua run several times a day, especially during peak tourist seasons.

The journey typically takes around two hours to reach Peso da Régua and slightly more to reach Pinhão.

It's wise to check the schedules ahead of time and purchase tickets early, particularly during harvest season when the valley gets busy.

9. Tips for Train Travelers

Opt for window seats on the right side when departing from Porto for the best river views.

Consider buying a first-class ticket for a more spacious and comfortable ride without a significant price difference.

Bring snacks and water, as some smaller stations and trains have limited services.

By Car: Driving Directions and Tips

Driving to the Douro Valley offers the ultimate flexibility and the chance to explore hidden gems off the beaten path. The drive itself is part of the adventure, winding through lush landscapes and scenic villages.

10. Driving from Porto

Starting from Porto, the most straightforward route is via the A4 highway heading east toward Amarante. From Amarante, follow signs toward Peso da Régua and the heart of the Douro Valley. The total drive takes approximately 1.5 to 2 hours, depending on traffic and your exact destination.

11. Driving from Lisbon

If you are coming from Lisbon, take the A1 highway north toward Porto, and then connect to the A4. While this journey is longer (around 4–5 hours), it offers the opportunity to explore central Portugal along the way if you wish to make stops.

12. Scenic Routes

For travelers who want to soak in the valley's grandeur, consider the N222 road between Peso da Régua and Pinhão. This road is often celebrated as one of the most beautiful drives in the world, tracing the river's curves and passing countless vineyards and quintas (wine estates).

Reaching the Douro Valley is part of the magic of visiting this unforgettable region. Whether you choose to soar into Porto and connect by train, cruise along scenic highways by car, or weave through vineyards aboard a charming train, every journey offers its own unique memories. Each route into the valley is laced with anticipation, revealing a land where time seems to slow, and every turn offers a new vista to treasure.

Chapter 3

Ideal Seasons Tourists Should Visit Douro Valley

The Douro Valley, with its serpentine river, terraced vineyards, and quaint villages, is a destination that changes personality with every season. Choosing the right time to visit can shape a traveler's experience dramatically. Here's a detailed breakdown of the ideal seasons to explore this timeless region.

1. Spring Awakening (March to May)

As winter recedes, the Douro Valley bursts back to life in spring, offering a soft and refreshing charm. March through May paints the landscape in every imaginable shade of green. The almond trees blossom, covering the hillsides with delicate white and pink flowers, creating an enchanting scenery.

During this period, the temperatures are moderate, usually sitting comfortably between 15°C and 22°C (59°F to 72°F). The air feels crisp, the skies are often clear, and the crowds are thinner compared to summer months. This combination makes it an ideal time for travelers who prefer peaceful boat rides along the river or scenic train journeys through the valley.

Vineyards begin to sprout vibrant leaves, and the wineries slowly stir from their winter rest. It's a wonderful season for wine enthusiasts eager to explore the estates before the busy harvest months. Hiking trails like the ones near Peso da Régua or Pinhão are perfect for those who want to enjoy the valley's natural beauty without the intense summer heat.

2. Early Summer Elegance (June)

Before the intense heat of high summer settles over the valley, June offers a sweet spot for visitors. The days grow longer, providing more sunlight to explore the region's riches. Wildflowers still linger along the riverbanks, and the vines thicken into lush canopies.

Temperatures in June typically hover around 25°C (77°F), warm enough to bask in the sun but not so hot as to make walking tours uncomfortable. This is the perfect month to indulge in outdoor picnics overlooking the valley or to take leisurely drives through the winding country roads that connect the charming villages.

The river becomes livelier during this time, and river cruises from Peso da Régua to Porto are especially pleasant. The summer festivities begin to trickle in, offering tourists a chance to witness local traditions without being overwhelmed by tourist throngs.

3. The Harvest Glory of Autumn (September to October)

If there is one time that truly defines the Douro Valley, it is the harvest season. September and October transform the region into a living, breathing painting. The vineyards shimmer in hues of gold, copper, and deep crimson, making it a paradise for photographers, nature lovers, and romantics alike.

This period is particularly special because visitors can witness — and even participate in — the traditional grape harvest, known as "vindima." Many quintas (wine estates) invite tourists to experience grape picking and the age-old custom of grape stomping, providing unforgettable memories.

Temperatures during these months remain agreeable, ranging from 18°C to 25°C (64°F to 77°F). The valley hums with excitement as workers gather grapes that will soon become the region's celebrated Port and table wines. Vineyards often host harvest festivals featuring local food, folk music, and wine tastings. It's an intoxicating time — in every sense of the word — to visit.

Furthermore, the sunsets during autumn seem almost exaggerated, splashing the river and hills with golden light that feels almost surreal. Every evening stroll feels cinematic, and every photograph looks like a masterpiece.

4. The Mild Winter Charm (November to February)

Although winter is the quietest season in the Douro Valley, it offers a certain understated beauty that often gets overlooked. November through February brings a hushed, reflective atmosphere to the valley, wrapping it in mists and cool breezes.

While temperatures can dip to 5°C (41°F) at night and hover around 12°C to 16°C (54°F to 61°F) during the day, they remain mild compared to much of Europe. Snow is rare, but when it dusts the mountaintops, the views are nothing short of breathtaking.

For travelers seeking solitude and authenticity, winter is a hidden gem. Cozying up by a fireplace in a traditional quinta, sipping vintage Port, and watching the morning fog roll across the river are experiences that few tourists get to savor. Accommodation rates are often lower, and restaurants and tasting rooms feel more intimate and personal.

It's also a wonderful time to explore the cultural side of the Douro. The historic towns of Lamego and Vila Real, with their ornate churches and palaces, are free from the bustle. Museums and local markets offer genuine interactions with residents, making a winter journey deeply enriching.

Every Season Tells a Different Story

There is no universally "perfect" season to visit the Douro Valley — only the one that best matches the traveler's desires. Whether drawn to the valley's springtime freshness, the sun-drenched early summer, the golden blaze of harvest, or the introspective quiet of winter, every visitor finds their own version of paradise.

Ultimately, the best time to visit hinges on what one wishes to experience. Spring and early summer are perfect for nature enthusiasts and active explorers. Autumn caters to wine lovers and photographers yearning for vivid scenery and cultural experiences. Winter speaks to those seeking tranquility, authenticity, and heartfelt connections.

One thing is certain: whenever you choose to go, the Douro Valley's magic will linger long after you leave — like the lingering notes of a fine, aged Port wine.

Festivals and Events in Douro Valley

1. Festa das Vindimas (Grape Harvest Festival)

The Grape Harvest Festival, known locally as Festa das Vindimas, is one of the most iconic events in the Douro Valley. Taking place every September, it celebrates the grape harvest that has shaped the region's life and economy for centuries. Villages and vineyards buzz with activity as locals and visitors join in picking grapes, stomping them barefoot in traditional stone tanks (lagares), and singing old harvest songs.

Many quintas (wine estates) open their doors to tourists, offering grape-picking experiences, guided tours, and rustic meals paired with excellent wines. The air fills with joy, the clinking of glasses, and the pride of a tradition deeply rooted in Douro soil.

2. São João Festival in Peso da Régua

While Porto's São João Festival is internationally famous, Peso da Régua — the Douro Valley's unofficial capital — hosts its own vibrant version. Celebrated in late June, this festival honors Saint John with colorful street decorations, parades, fireworks, and lively music performances.

A charming custom is the playful act of hitting friends and strangers alike on the head with soft plastic hammers or fragrant garlic flowers. The town's riverbanks become the epicenter of parties, grilled sardines, and folk dances that stretch into the early morning hours.

3. Douro Film Harvest

Cinema lovers find a hidden gem in the Douro Film Harvest, an event dedicated to celebrating cinema, wine, and gastronomy. Held usually in the fall, the festival draws filmmakers, actors, wine enthusiasts, and travelers to various charming venues across the Douro Valley. Outdoor screenings, exclusive wine tastings, and gourmet food pairings create a unique atmosphere where the arts and Douro's natural beauty blend effortlessly. It's not just about watching films; it's about savoring experiences in breathtaking settings.

4. Festival de Sabores do Douro

Food is another vital heartbeat of the Douro Valley, and the Festival de Sabores do Douro showcases the region's rich culinary heritage. Typically hosted during the winter months, this event gathers artisans, farmers, and chefs to present their best products. Hearty dishes like posta mirandesa (a thick grilled beef steak) and creamy rice with smoked sausages are highlights. Visitors can sample dozens of regional specialties, from honey and olive oil to dried fruits and handcrafted sweets, all while enjoying traditional folk music performances.

5. Romaria de Nossa Senhora dos Remédios

One of the grandest religious pilgrimages in northern Portugal, the Romaria de Nossa Senhora dos Remédios transforms the town of Lamego each September. Over several days, the town dresses in festive lights and colorful banners. Religious processions, concerts, fireworks, and street fairs all converge to honor the Virgin Mary. A moving moment is the penitential climb of pilgrims up the monumental staircase of the Sanctuary of Our Lady of Remedies, often on their knees as a form of devotion. Whether religious or not, visitors find the atmosphere touching and the town's energy contagious.

6. Festa da Cereja (Cherry Festival) in Resende

As spring colors the valley with life, Resende, a town known for its luscious cherries, holds its Cherry Festival. Typically taking place in May, the festival celebrates the arrival of the juicy fruit season. Streets and market squares overflow with cherry stalls, and visitors are encouraged to taste, buy, and even pick cherries directly from orchards. Live music, folklore groups, and cooking demonstrations using cherries as a star ingredient add a vibrant layer to the experience.

7. Régua Wine Fest

For wine aficionados, Régua Wine Fest is a dream event, merging the rich tradition of Douro winemaking with contemporary flair. Set along the riverfront of Peso da Régua during the summer months, this festival offers extensive wine tastings, music concerts, workshops, and art exhibitions. Young winemakers share the spotlight with established estates, and visitors can enjoy masterclasses in wine pairing and sensory analysis. As the sun sets behind the hills, the open-air parties begin, filling the night with laughter and clinking glasses.

8. Corgo Fest

In Vila Real, the lively Corgo Fest brings together music, art, and gastronomy in an energetic weekend event. Emerging as a fresh take on traditional festivals, Corgo Fest usually features a vibrant lineup of contemporary musicians, DJs, art installations, food trucks, and craft beer stands. Families and groups of friends gather in parks and riverside areas, making it a laid-back yet thrilling experience. It's a great opportunity to see the younger, creative side of the Douro Valley.

9. Festa de São Bartolomeu in Torre de Moncorvo

Every August, the small but spirited town of Torre de Moncorvo celebrates the Festa de São Bartolomeu with processions, bull-running events, traditional music, and local markets. This centuries-old festival ties together religious devotion and rustic entertainment. Artisans display their handmade goods, from pottery to woven baskets, and the streets fill with people enjoying roasted chestnuts, cured meats, and generous glasses of local wine.

10. Festival Douro Blues

Music lovers rejoice at Festival Douro Blues, a niche but growing event dedicated to the blues genre. Typically staged in historic venues like wine cellars and old manor houses, the festival attracts both Portuguese and international artists. Intimate concerts, jam sessions, and blues-themed dinners create an atmosphere of relaxed sophistication. It's a musical journey that resonates beautifully with the slow rhythms of the Douro River.

The Douro Valley's festivals and events are not merely spectacles; they are immersive invitations into the soul of the region. Every celebration, whether grand or humble, tells a story of heritage, resilience, and joy. From the rhythm of grape harvests to the melodies of riverfront concerts, the valley offers countless moments where visitors can feel not like outsiders, but welcomed guests sharing in age-old traditions.

Timing a visit to coincide with one or more of these events promises deeper connections, richer memories, and a more intimate understanding of this mesmerizing landscape.

Douro Valley Travel Guide 2025

Chapter 4

Accommodation Options for Tourists in Douro Valley: Top 10 Hotels to Stay

Finding the perfect place to stay can turn a Douro Valley journey into an unforgettable experience. Whether you're seeking vineyard vistas, riverfront luxury, or charming countryside retreats, the Douro offers something for every taste and budget. Below, you'll discover the top ten places to call home during your exploration of this lush, captivating region.

1. Quinta do Sol Vineyard Estate

- Address: Estrada Nacional 222, Peso da Régua
- Price per Night: €220

Tucked among rolling vineyards and golden hills, Quinta do Sol offers a boutique stay that blends rustic charm with understated luxury. Each room overlooks sun-drenched terraces or the winding Douro River. Guests can savor homegrown wines, wander through olive groves, or simply lounge by the infinity pool, glass of port in hand.

Douro Valley Travel Guide 2025

2. River's Embrace Hotel

- Address: Rua da Ribeira, Pinhão
- Price per Night: €195

If waking up to the gentle whispers of the river is your dream, River's Embrace Hotel will sweep you off your feet. Set directly along the Douro's edge, the hotel offers modern yet cozy rooms, an open-air restaurant, and boat tours that glide across the shimmering waters. Expect warm hospitality wrapped in natural beauty.

3. Casa do Miradouro Boutique Inn

- Address: Rua Alto do Miradouro, São João da Pesqueira
- Price per Night: €140

Casa do Miradouro lives up to its name — "House of the Viewpoint" — by offering mesmerizing panoramas across vine-laden hills. With just ten intimate rooms, this boutique inn promises serenity. Its sun-kissed terraces and hearty breakfasts filled with regional flavors make it a perfect hideaway for travelers craving authenticity.

4. Palácio Douro Elegance

- Address: Avenida Central, Lamego

- Price per Night: €260

Housed in a meticulously restored 19th-century palace, Palácio Douro Elegance drips with sophistication. High ceilings, ornate chandeliers, and frescoed salons transport guests back to a more romantic era. The spa, set in the former royal wine cellars, offers vinotherapy treatments that pamper body and soul after a day of exploration.

5. Vale Encantado Rural Lodge

- Address: Caminho das Vinhas, Armamar
- Price per Night: €110

For those yearning for peace amid nature, Vale Encantado — or "Enchanted Valley" — Lodge is a dream come true. Surrounded by terraced vineyards and ancient olive trees, it offers charming cottages with wood-burning fireplaces, hammocks under fig trees, and homemade jams served at breakfast. A retreat for the soul.

6. Douro Vista River Resort

- Address: Marginal do Douro, Peso da Régua
- Price per Night: €230

Douro Vista is ideal for travelers who love a blend of leisure and luxury. With its panoramic rooftop pool, riverside dining, and spa treatments using local grape extracts, it brings a contemporary flair to the Douro's ancient heart. The suites feature floor-to-ceiling windows that flood the rooms with golden sunlight.

7. Casa das Flores Heritage Hotel

- Address: Travessa das Flores, Pinhão
- Price per Night: €175

Bursting with character, Casa das Flores is nestled within Pinhão's historic district. Each room tells a story through antique furniture, handwoven linens, and artisanal décor. Guests often linger in the jasmine-scented courtyard where breakfast — featuring flaky pastries and rich local honey — is served under a canopy of wisteria.

8. Encosta do Rio Eco-Lodge

- Address: Estrada do Rio, Vila Real
- Price per Night: €150

For the eco-conscious traveler, Encosta do Rio is a treasure trove. Built entirely with sustainable materials, the lodge offers solar-powered suites, organic farm-to-table meals, and nature walks that invite you to reconnect with the land. The soothing soundtrack of flowing water and birdsong is included free of charge.

9. Solar dos Nobres Wine Hotel

- Address: Rua dos Nobres, Sabrosa
- Price per Night: €200

Solar dos Nobres is a celebration of the Douro's wine making legacy. Guests can sleep surrounded by ancient vineyards, enjoy private tastings in vaulted cellars, and join grape-harvesting festivities during the vendimia season. Its regal interiors, from carved oak headboards to tapestries, create a rich, welcoming atmosphere.

10. Quinta da Aurora Country House

- Address: Caminho da Aurora, Tabuaço
- Price per Night: €125

At Quinta da Aurora, simplicity shines. This country house exudes warmth, with terracotta floors, cozy reading nooks, and gardens bursting with lavender and rosemary. After a day exploring riverside villages, guests can gather around the outdoor fireplace, swapping stories beneath a star-blanketed sky.

Transportation Options within Douro Valley: Routes, Prices, and Real-Life Examples

1. Train Travel – The Classic Douro Route

One of the most memorable ways to explore Douro Valley is by train. The Linha do Douro (Douro Line) connects Porto to Pocinho, slicing through some of the most jaw-dropping scenery imaginable.

Route:
The journey starts at Porto's São Bento Station, moving eastward toward Régua, Pinhão, and finally Pocinho. The highlight is the stretch between Régua and Pinhão, where the train snakes along the riverbanks with endless vineyards on both sides.

Price Range:

Porto to Régua: Around €10-€12 one-way.

Porto to Pinhão: Around €11-€13 one-way.

Full ride to Pocinho: About €13-€15 one-way.

Example:
Imagine boarding an early morning train from Porto, coffee in hand, as the sunrise bathes the valley in gold. For about €12, you can sit back in a vintage-style carriage and be hypnotized by vine-covered hills without worrying about winding mountain roads.

Pro Tip:
Always sit on the right-hand side of the train when heading east from Porto — the best river views are on that side.

2. Rental Car – Freedom to Roam

For travelers who cherish flexibility, renting a car is a brilliant choice. With your own wheels, you can dip into sleepy villages, hidden quintas (wine estates), and secluded viewpoints that no bus or train will ever reach.

Route:
Popular driving itineraries include:

Porto → Peso da Régua → Pinhão → São João da Pesqueira.

Pinhão → Provesende → Alijó for wine country adventures.

Price Range:

Daily rental: €40-€70 for a compact car.

Fuel costs: Expect about €1.80 per liter, and a full day of touring might cost €20-€30 in gas.

Example:
Think of cruising along N222, famously dubbed "the most beautiful road in the world," with windows down, the scent of ripening grapes in the air, and spontaneous stops at family-owned wineries for tastings. For around €100 (car + gas), you get complete control over your day.

Pro Tip:
Some roads are narrow and winding — choose a smaller car for easier navigation and parking.

3. River Cruises – Sail Through the Heart of the Valley

For a leisurely, romantic exploration, nothing beats a river cruise along the Douro. It's the original highway of the valley, once used to transport barrels of Port wine to Porto.

Douro Valley Travel Guide 2025

Route:

Porto to Régua (day cruises)

Régua to Pinhão (shorter, scenic cruises)

Longer itineraries can reach all the way to Barca d'Alva near the Spanish border.

Price Range:

Half-day cruises: €30-€50.

Full-day cruises (with meals): €70-€120.

Multi-day luxury cruises: €500-€1500 depending on the duration and amenities.

Example:
Picture yourself on a traditional rabelo boat, gliding past vineyards that tumble down to the water's edge. With a glass of local wine in hand and a regional lunch included, a day cruise from Régua to Pinhão for around €80 feels like a scene straight out of a travel magazine.

Pro Tip:
Reserve cruises in advance, especially in peak months (May–September), as they fill up quickly.

4. Private Transfers – Comfort Without Hassle

If you crave comfort but don't want to drive, hiring a private transfer is the middle ground between adventure and ease. A driver picks you up and handles the winding roads while you soak in the views.

Route:
Common transfers include:

Porto to Régua

Porto to Pinhão

Custom wine tours across multiple estates

Price Range:

One-way transfer from Porto to Pinhão: €120-€150 per car (up to 4 people).

Full-day chauffeur services: around €250-€350 depending on stops and hours.

Example:
Envision being whisked from your Porto hotel to a boutique vineyard near Pinhão without lifting a finger. A

family of four could split a €140 ride, making it only €35 per person — a perfect blend of luxury and practicality.

Pro Tip:
Some drivers double as local guides, offering insider stories about the valley's traditions and wineries. Always ask!

5. Biking – For the Adventurous Spirits

Cycling through Douro Valley is not for the faint-hearted, but it's absolutely unforgettable for active travelers who want to be in the landscape, not just looking at it.

Route:

Pinhão to Provesende: A challenging yet rewarding climb.

Régua riverside paths: Flatter and suitable for intermediate bikers.

Price Range:

Bike rentals: €20-€30 per day.

Guided bike tours: €60-€100 per day (often including bike, guide, and picnic).

Example:
Imagine pedaling through a vine-scented morning mist, passing through villages where locals wave hello. Renting a mountain bike in Pinhão for €25 lets you independently explore terraced hillsides few tourists ever see.

Pro Tip:
Summer heat can be brutal; start early and carry plenty of water. Always wear a helmet — some roads are shared with cars and trucks.

6. Public Buses – Economical but Limited

If you're on a strict budget, public buses offer an affordable, though less flexible, way to travel between towns in Douro Valley.

Route:

Porto to Peso da Régua

Régua to Lamego, Pinhão, Vila Real

Douro Valley Travel Guide 2025

Price Range:

Porto to Régua: €8-€10.

Short hops between valley towns: €2-€5.

Example:
A backpacker could catch a morning bus from Porto to Régua for just €9, saving their euros for vineyard visits and tastings. While it's not glamorous and requires patience, it's a solid option for slow travelers.

Pro Tip:
Bus schedules can be sparse, especially on weekends. Always check timetables carefully and don't expect English-speaking drivers — having your destination written down helps.

7. Walking – For the Soulful Explorers

For the purists who believe journeys are meant to be slow and soulful, walking through parts of Douro Valley is a spiritual experience.

Route:

Pinhão to Casal de Loivos: A famous short hike (~6km round trip).

Douro Valley Travel Guide 2025

Longer village-to-village trails are also marked, especially near Provesende and Alijó.

Price Range:

Free! Just invest in good hiking shoes, water, and maybe a taxi back if needed.

Example:
Imagine hiking from Pinhão uphill to Casal de Loivos. After a sweaty climb, you're rewarded with one of the most jaw-dropping views over the entire valley — and it costs you nothing but effort.

Pro Tip:
Maps are available at local tourism offices. Always check weather forecasts; storms can roll in unexpectedly during spring and autumn.

Chapter 5

Beaches in Douro Valley for Tourists to Explore

Though the Douro Valley is celebrated worldwide for its undulating vineyards and ancient wine estates, it also hides a collection of river beaches perfect for travelers seeking a serene escape. These beaches along the Douro River offer refreshing waters, idyllic scenery, and authentic Portuguese charm.

1. Praia Fluvial de Lomba

Tucked in the municipality of Baião, Praia Fluvial de Lomba is a dreamy spot where tourists can immerse themselves in the tranquil waters of the Douro. Encircled by lush hills and stone terraces, the beach feels like a secret haven.

Location: Baião, about 80 km east of Porto

Entry Price: Free

Entry Requirements: No special requirements; open access to all visitors.

The beach offers grassy banks for sunbathing, picnic areas, and a small bar for light refreshments. Lifeguards are often present during peak summer months, adding a layer of safety for families with children.

2. Praia Fluvial de Bitetos

Nestled beside an ancient monastery, Praia Fluvial de Bitetos combines history with natural beauty. The river here runs deep and still, making it ideal for swimming and kayaking.

Location: Penafiel, close to Entre-os-Rios

Entry Price: Free

Entry Requirements: No permits needed; suitable for all ages.

This beach is well-equipped with shaded picnic spots, a café serving local snacks, and kayak rentals. Many tourists choose to stop here on their way to wine tours, making it a delightful dual experience.

3. Praia Fluvial da Congida

If you wander further east near Freixo de Espada à Cinta, you'll find the spectacular Praia Fluvial da Congida. The river here widens magnificently, creating a vast and calm swimming area embraced by rugged cliffs.

Location: Freixo de Espada à Cinta, northeastern Douro Valley

Entry Price: Free

Entry Requirements: None, although swimmers are advised to stay within the marked areas for safety.

Facilities include a floating pool on the river, changing rooms, shaded areas, and a charming riverside café. In the summer, local festivals often add a lively atmosphere to this otherwise quiet beach.

4. Praia Fluvial do Areinho

Located near the town of Arouca, Praia Fluvial do Areinho sits on the margins of the Paiva River, one of Douro's tributaries. This beach is a perfect launching point for visitors aiming to walk the famous Paiva Walkways.

Location: Arouca Municipality

Douro Valley Travel Guide 2025

Entry Price: Around €2 per person (for parking and maintenance fees)

Entry Requirements: No special documents needed; parking fees apply.

Areinho is known for its fine golden sands, crystal-clear waters, and picnic-friendly environment. Adventurous tourists often pair a visit to the beach with a walk across the world's longest pedestrian suspension bridge nearby.

5. Praia Fluvial de Porto de Rei

Porto de Rei offers an intimate experience for travelers looking to dive deeper into local life. This modest yet charming river beach is less touristy than others, making it ideal for a peaceful afternoon.

Location: Resende, Viseu District

Entry Price: Free

Entry Requirements: Open to the public without any restrictions.

The beach features a small pier, calm waters for swimming, and a handful of family-run restaurants nearby offering hearty Portuguese meals. It's a hidden jewel worth discovering if you prefer off-the-beaten-path experiences.

6. Praia Fluvial da Senhora da Ribeira

This secluded river beach near the medieval village of Carrazeda de Ansiães offers an enchanting experience where history and nature intertwine.

Location: Carrazeda de Ansiães, Bragança District

Entry Price: Free

Entry Requirements: Open access.

Praia da Senhora da Ribeira charms visitors with its smooth pebbly shores, expansive green spaces for lounging, and breathtaking sunset views. It's particularly popular among camping enthusiasts, as a small camping park operates adjacent to the beach.

7. Praia Fluvial de Samouco

A quieter spot along the Douro River, Praia Fluvial de Samouco, invites travelers looking for undisturbed tranquility amid scenic beauty.

Douro Valley Travel Guide 2025

Location: Near Vila Nova de Foz Côa

Entry Price: Free

Entry Requirements: No special requirements.

This beach offers basic amenities like shaded rest spots and clear, cool waters ideal for a lazy swim. The area's proximity to prehistoric rock art sites also makes it a cultural hotbed for curious tourists.

8. Praia Fluvial de Caldas de Aregos

Located by the thermal springs of Caldas de Aregos, this beach combines river swimming with wellness tourism.

Location: Resende Municipality

Entry Price: Free for beach access; optional fees for spa services

Entry Requirements: No beach restrictions, but spa facilities require reservations and payment.

Many visitors enjoy a morning swim followed by a rejuvenating spa treatment, creating a luxurious day of relaxation framed by the hills of Douro.

9. Praia Fluvial de Sebadelhe

This river beach, although smaller than others, captivates visitors with its untouched scenery and peaceful environment.

Location: Sebadelhe, Vila Nova de Foz Côa

Entry Price: Free

Entry Requirements: Open access.

There are limited facilities here, but the setting compensates beautifully — towering trees, chirping birds, and the gentle sound of flowing water create a perfect nature escape.

10. Praia Fluvial do Castelo

One of the lesser-known gems, Praia Fluvial do Castelo, sits next to a crumbling medieval tower, offering a sense of historic mystery with every visit.

Location: Near Mesão Frio

Entry Price: Free

Entry Requirements: No entry barriers; visitors must respect preservation signs near historical structures.

Historical Sites and Monuments in Douro Valley

1. Lamego Cathedral (Sé de Lamego)

One of the crown jewels of the Douro Valley, Lamego Cathedral is an exquisite embodiment of centuries of architectural evolution. Originally constructed in the 12th century, it boasts a mesmerizing combination of Romanesque roots with later Gothic, Renaissance, and Baroque influences.

Tourists arriving in the city of Lamego will find the cathedral at the heart of the old town, easily accessible on foot from the main avenue. Visitors often begin their exploration at the magnificent bell tower, one of the few remnants from the medieval structure. As you step inside, the richly adorned nave, intricate wooden choir stalls, and the beautiful frescoes on the ceilings will instantly transport you to another era. Many choose to join guided walking tours starting from the Lamego Museum to the Cathedral for a seamless historical experience.

2. Sanctuary of Nossa Senhora dos Remédios

No visit to the Douro is complete without witnessing the sheer splendor of the Sanctuary of Nossa Senhora dos Remédios, perched elegantly above Lamego. Built between the 18th and 20th centuries, this monumental baroque shrine is both a spiritual retreat and a visual marvel.

Visitors typically ascend the legendary 686-step staircase, lined with beautifully tiled panels (azulejos) depicting religious scenes and ornate fountains. For those who prefer a less strenuous route, taxis or tuk-tuks from Lamego's town center provide a direct ride to the sanctuary's summit. Once at the top, the panoramic views of Lamego's rooftops and the distant Douro hills reward every traveler's efforts.

3. Castelo de Numão

Nestled in the tranquil village of Numão, this medieval fortress is an overlooked gem of the Douro region. Castelo de Numão was originally built by the Moors and later expanded by Christian forces after the Reconquista.

Tourists keen to experience authentic, off-the-beaten-path history will find the castle after a scenic drive through winding vineyard roads. A short, moderate hike from the village center leads up to the castle ruins. Once there, visitors can roam freely among the crumbling walls and ancient stone watchtowers, all while enjoying sweeping views of the valley and nearby archaeological sites.

4. Mateus Palace (Solar de Mateus)

Although technically just outside the traditional Douro wine-producing zone, Mateus Palace near Vila Real is an architectural masterpiece too captivating to ignore. This 18th-century baroque manor is famously depicted on the label of the Mateus rosé wine.

To explore Mateus Palace, travelers usually book a guided tour that delves into the palace's history, from its aristocratic owners to its artistic treasures. The lush gardens, reflective ponds, and ornate interiors feel like stepping into a noble's secret world. Public buses and taxis from Vila Real's center make reaching the palace straightforward for those without a car.

5. Romanesque Churches of the Douro Valley

The Douro Valley is sprinkled with petite yet magnificent Romanesque churches dating back to the 11th and 12th centuries. Each one holds silent testimony to the region's deep religious and cultural heritage.

Some standout examples include:

Church of São Pedro de Balsemão, reputedly one of Portugal's oldest Christian temples.

Church of São Martinho de Mouros, with its stark, fortress-like facade.

Travelers often embark on thematic "Romanesque Route" tours, offered by local guides, which provide transport and insightful commentary between the churches. Renting a car also grants visitors the flexibility to explore these hidden gems at their own pace, with scenic drives along the riverbanks.

6. Castelo de Ansiães

Standing lonely but proud atop a rugged hill near Carrazeda de Ansiães, the Castle of Ansiães tells stories of conquest, defense, and abandonment. With roots stretching back to Roman times, this fortified settlement later became an important medieval stronghold.

Tourists generally drive to a designated parking area and then hike a marked trail up to the fortress. The walk is relatively easy and richly rewarding, offering commanding views over ancient terraces and olive groves. Interpretation panels in English and Portuguese along the trail help visitors imagine life during the castle's golden era.

7. Monastery of Salzedas

Deep in the Tarouca municipality lies the hauntingly beautiful Monastery of Salzedas, founded in the 12th century by Cistercian monks. Its partial ruins evoke a sense of quiet reverence, with towering Gothic arches and delicate stone carvings hinting at its former grandeur.

Visitors usually join small group tours, available from Tarouca town, which often combine Salzedas with a visit to the nearby Monastery of São João de Tarouca. Walking through Salzedas' massive cloister, crumbling refectory, and solemn church, travelers feel the passage of centuries in every creak and echo.

8. Archaeological Park of the Côa Valley

For those seeking a more ancient connection, the Côa Valley Archaeological Park offers one of the world's most significant collections of open-air prehistoric rock art, dating back 25,000 years.

Tourists must book official guided tours through the park's visitor center in Vila Nova de Foz Côa, as independent visits to the rock sites are not permitted. The tours include 4x4 vehicle rides across rugged terrain, leading visitors to see ancient engravings of horses, aurochs, and human figures carved into stone cliffs — a profoundly moving glimpse into humanity's earliest artistry.

9. Torre de Moncorvo

The charming town of Torre de Moncorvo boasts one of the largest parish churches in Portugal, the Church of Nossa Senhora da Assunção. This Gothic-Renaissance masterpiece is affectionately known as the "Stone Cathedral."

Travelers usually stroll from the town's quaint central square to the church, admiring the intricately carved main portal and robust bell towers along the way. Inside, the golden altarpiece and expansive vaulted ceilings leave a lasting impression on all who enter. Many visitors enjoy combining a tour of the church with leisurely café stops in Moncorvo's sun-drenched streets.

10. Medieval Bridge of Ucanha

Last but not least, the Medieval Bridge of Ucanha is a remarkable example of fortified bridge architecture, originally built to collect tolls from travelers crossing the river Varosa.

Outdoor Activities for Tourists to Explore in Douro Valley

1. Wine Estate Tours and Vineyard Walks

One cannot visit the Douro Valley without walking through its heart—the vineyards. Across the hillsides, rows of grapevines weave intricate patterns, and many quintas (wine estates) open their doors for immersive vineyard tours. Visitors can stroll along narrow, winding paths between vines heavy with grapes, absorbing centuries-old viticulture traditions.

For example, a walk through Quinta do Seixo offers a captivating blend of nature and heritage, often ending with a tasting session under shaded pergolas. Some estates, like Quinta da Pacheca, even allow guests to participate in grape harvesting during harvest season, making the experience both tactile and memorable.

2. Douro River Cruises

Douro Valley Travel Guide 2025

Gliding along the Douro River unveils the valley from a new and serene perspective. Whether aboard a traditional rabelo boat or a sleek modern yacht, river cruises allow tourists to marvel at towering cliffs, lush vineyards, and quaint villages lining the banks.

Short trips between Peso da Régua and Pinhão showcase the heart of the valley, while longer day cruises extend all the way to Porto. Aboard these boats, visitors often enjoy local wines and gourmet lunches, transforming a scenic ride into an indulgent, slow-paced celebration of the valley's beauty.

3. Hiking Through the Vineyards and Hills

For those eager to lace up their boots, the Douro Valley presents countless hiking opportunities. Trails snake through terraced vineyards, olive groves, and sleepy hamlets, offering hikers dramatic vistas at every turn.

A notable example is the São Leonardo da Galafura Trail, where a climb up to the viewpoint rewards trekkers with sweeping views of the river winding through the hills. Another popular route leads from Pinhão to Casal de Loivos, a moderately challenging path culminating in one of the most photogenic overlooks of the valley.

4. Cycling Along the Douro Roads

Douro Valley Travel Guide 2025

The winding country roads and riverside paths make the Douro Valley a paradise for cycling enthusiasts. Riding a bike allows tourists to cover more ground while still savoring the changing landscapes up close.

Renting an electric bike in Peso da Régua, for example, enables even casual riders to explore the valley's undulating terrain without exhaustion. For more adventurous spirits, a cycle from Peso da Régua to Vila Real combines challenging climbs with stunning mountain views. Many bike rental companies also offer guided tours, ensuring cyclists don't miss hidden gems along the way.

5. Hot Air Balloon Rides

Few experiences compare to the breathtaking serenity of drifting above the Douro Valley in a hot air balloon. As the balloon ascends, the patchwork of vineyards, the snaking river, and the misty mountains unfold beneath like a painting come to life.

Operators often launch at sunrise, when the light paints the valley in golden hues. Flights typically last about an hour, and after touching down, it's common to celebrate with a glass of local sparkling wine—a fitting toast to an unforgettable adventure.

Douro Valley Travel Guide 2025

6. Kayaking and Canoeing on the Douro

For water lovers, kayaking or canoeing along the Douro River offers an intimate way to interact with the valley's natural beauty. Paddlers can glide past secluded riverbanks, under historic bridges, and alongside ancient terraced vineyards.

A popular route is between Pinhão and Tua, where the water is calm, and the landscapes are spellbinding. Guided tours often include picnic stops at river islands, where travelers can savor local cheeses and wines, turning a sporty excursion into a sensory feast.

7. Birdwatching and Wildlife Spotting

Beyond its vineyards, the Douro Valley harbors a surprising array of wildlife. Birdwatchers can spot species such as the black kite, griffon vulture, and the dazzling European bee-eater, especially in the rugged eastern reaches near the Douro International Natural Park.

Organized wildlife tours provide insight into the valley's ecological diversity. For instance, visitors might join a local guide for an early morning hike, where the silence is broken only by birdsong and the occasional rustle of a fox in the brush. Such encounters deepen one's appreciation for the valley's untamed corners.

8. Visiting Historic Villages and Castles

Scattered across the hillsides are villages where time seems to have paused. Exploring these cobbled streets and ancient fortresses is like stepping into the past.

The village of Provesende, with its baroque mansions and sleepy squares, invites slow wandering. Nearby, the Castle of Numão offers panoramic views and an aura of mystery, with crumbling walls whispering stories of medieval skirmishes. Each stop provides a glimpse into the valley's layered history, blending human ingenuity with natural splendor.

9. Horseback Riding Tours

For a timeless and romantic way to experience the Douro, many travelers opt for horseback riding tours through the countryside. Trotting along sun-dappled trails through olive groves and vineyards, riders feel intimately connected to the landscape.

Ranches around Peso da Régua and Lamego offer guided rides tailored to all experience levels. Beginners can enjoy gentle riverbank paths, while seasoned riders might embark on longer treks into the hills, perhaps ending the day with a picnic and wine tasting under an ancient cork oak.

10. Picnicking Amidst the Vineyards

Sometimes, the simplest activities bring the greatest joy. Many estates and local companies now offer picnic experiences where guests receive a basket brimming with regional delights—fresh breads, cheeses, cured meats, and, naturally, a bottle of Douro wine.

One delightful spot for a picnic is the terrace gardens of Quinta Nova de Nossa Senhora do Carmo, where one can dine amidst the vines with the river shimmering in the distance. It's a moment to savor the slow, rich pace of life that defines the valley.

11. Stand-Up Paddleboarding (SUP) Adventures

Adventurers seeking a novel water activity often turn to stand-up paddleboarding. While the Douro River is broad and deep, many calmer stretches around Peso da Régua and Pinhão are ideal for paddleboarding.

Gliding quietly across the surface allows participants to enjoy an unhurried communion with the landscape. Many rental services also organize SUP tours at sunrise or sunset, when the valley is bathed in a magical light, enhancing the peacefulness of the experience.

12. Jeep Safaris and Off-Road Tours

For those who want to explore rugged terrain without hiking, jeep safaris offer a thrilling alternative. These tours bounce across the backroads and dusty tracks that weave through the less accessible parts of the Douro Valley.

One popular route takes visitors into the International Douro Natural Park, revealing dramatic cliffs, deep gorges, and traditional villages far off the beaten path. Guides often weave storytelling into the ride, sharing legends and secrets that make the dusty ride a narrative adventure as well.

13. Fishing in the Douro River

The Douro River is not just for sightseeing; it's also a rewarding fishing destination. Anglers can cast their lines for species like barbel, carp, and shad, either from the riverbanks or aboard small boats.

Fishing licenses are easy to obtain, and many local guides offer packages that include equipment rental and insider knowledge on the best spots. Whether serious about the catch or simply wanting a peaceful few hours by the water, fishing offers a tranquil slice of Douro life.

Even amateur shutterbugs will find countless opportunities: reflections on the river, gnarled vines against stone walls, and panoramic landscapes from hilltop viewpoints. Some tours even incorporate short photography workshops, helping visitors take home stunning visual memories of their journey.

Chapter 6

Top Foods for Tourists in Douro Valley (and Their Health Benefits)

The Douro Valley isn't just a visual wonder of terraced vineyards and rolling hills — it's a culinary treasure chest brimming with unforgettable flavors. As you roam this picturesque region, you'll find a menu that blends tradition, passion, and an instinctive respect for nature. Here's a feast of the top foods you must savor during your Douro Valley adventure, along with the incredible health benefits tucked into each bite.

1. Posta Mirandesa (Grilled Beef Steak)

One cannot talk about Douro Valley cuisine without mentioning Posta Mirandesa — a thick, juicy slab of beef grilled to smoky perfection. Originating from the Mirandesa breed of cattle, this steak is known for its marbled tenderness.

Health Benefits:

Beef from Mirandesa cattle is naturally grass-fed, providing a rich source of high-quality protein, iron, and vitamin B12 — essential for energy, muscle repair, and healthy red blood cells. Thanks to its natural upbringing, the fat profile leans toward healthier omega-3 fatty acids compared to conventionally raised beef.

2. Bacalhau à Brás (Codfish Scramble)

Cod, or "bacalhau," is a sacred ingredient across Portugal, and the Douro Valley has its own love story with this salted fish. In the dish Bacalhau à Brás, shredded cod is tossed with thinly cut potatoes and silky eggs, then dusted with fresh herbs.

Health Benefits:

Cod is a lean fish packed with omega-3 fatty acids that boost heart health. It's also a fantastic source of selenium, an antioxidant mineral vital for thyroid function and cellular repair.

3. Alheira de Mirandela (Smoked Sausage)

Alheira is not your average sausage. Traditionally made from a mixture of poultry, bread, and garlic, this smoky delicacy carries a rich backstory and an even richer flavor.

Health Benefits:

Though hearty, alheira offers high-protein content essential for maintaining muscle mass. Garlic, a prominent ingredient, delivers allicin, a compound famed for its heart-protective and antimicrobial properties.

4. Cabrito Assado (Roasted Kid Goat)

If you seek something tender and aromatic, Cabrito Assado — slow-roasted kid goat — will be your calling. The meat is seasoned with local herbs and roasted until meltingly soft.

Health Benefits:

Goat meat is leaner than beef or pork, making it a lower-fat alternative for red meat lovers. It's also packed with potassium and zinc, supporting nerve function and immune strength.

5. Queijo da Serra (Mountain Cheese)

Cheese lovers, rejoice! Queijo da Serra is a semi-soft sheep's cheese with a buttery, slightly tangy flavor that speaks of the rugged highlands surrounding Douro.

Health Benefits:

Sheep's milk cheese offers a higher concentration of calcium and protein compared to cow's milk cheese. It's also rich in conjugated linoleic acid (CLA), a healthy fat linked to improved heart health and weight management.

6. Tripas à Moda do Porto (Porto-Style Tripé)

Though technically a dish more famous in Porto, its influence spills into the Douro region. Tripas à Moda do Porto features slow-cooked tripe with white beans and smoked meats.

Health Benefits:

Tripe is surprisingly rich in collagen, which promotes joint health and skin elasticity. It's also lower in fat than many traditional meats, making it a nutrient-dense but lighter option.

7. Rojões (Pork Bites)

Small cubes of pork, marinated and fried in their own juices, Rojões are a rustic comfort food often enjoyed during Douro festivities.

Health Benefits:

Pork, especially cuts used for rojões, provides B vitamins like thiamin and niacin, crucial for converting food into usable energy. When sourced from local farms, it's often less processed and free from additives.

8. Amêndoas de Douro (Douro Almonds)

While you might associate the Douro with grapes, almonds are another star crop here. Amêndoas de Douro — roasted or candied almonds — are a sweet, crunchy snack often enjoyed with port wine.

Health Benefits:

Almonds are nutritional powerhouses, boasting vitamin E, magnesium, and fiber. They promote heart health, aid digestion, and even support healthy skin.

9. Peixinhos da Horta (Vegetable Fritters)

This charming dish translates to "little fish of the garden," though there's no seafood involved. Green beans are battered and fried until golden, creating a crispy, addictive treat.

Health Benefits:

Despite being fried, green beans deliver a good dose of vitamin C, vitamin K, and antioxidants that fight inflammation and support bone health.

10. Lampreia à Bordalesa (Bordeaux-style Lamprey)

A seasonal delicacy, Lampreia is a jawless fish stewed with wine and spices. It's a bold culinary experience not for the faint of heart!

Health Benefits:

Lamprey meat is exceptionally high in iron and vitamin A, essential for blood health and vision. Its unique protein structure is also easier to digest for sensitive stomachs.

11. Pão de Ló (Sponge Cake)

No Douro Valley meal ends without a slice of Pão de Ló, an airy sponge cake that almost melts on your tongue, often slightly underbaked for extra gooeyness.

Health Benefits:

Made primarily with eggs, Pão de Ló is surprisingly rich in choline, a nutrient vital for brain function. It's a sweet indulgence but offers a whisper of nourishment.

12. Castanhas Assadas (Roasted Chestnuts)

In autumn, the Douro air fills with the smoky scent of roasted chestnuts — an age-old snack that feels like a hug from the earth.

Health Benefits:

Chestnuts are lower in fat than most other nuts and high in complex carbohydrates that offer a slow, steady release of energy. They're also a natural source of vitamin C.

Top Restaurants to Visit in Douro Valley with Their Signature Dishes

1. Quinta da Tábua – Savor the Roasted Goat

Hidden among the sloping vineyards, Quinta da Tábua offers a genuine taste of the Douro countryside. The star of their menu is the roasted goat with chestnuts, a dish slowly cooked in a wood-fired oven. The meat falls off the bone, bathed in a fragrant sauce that echoes with hints of rosemary and native herbs. Paired with their own house-made red wine, the experience feels like a cozy Sunday lunch at a Portuguese farmhouse.

Douro Valley Travel Guide 2025

2. Casa do Rio – Delight in Trout with Almond Crust

Located along the gleaming riverbanks, Casa do Rio perfectly merges nature and gastronomy. Their almond-crusted trout is a standout. Freshly caught from the Douro River, the fish is enrobed in a crispy, nutty shell and served atop a bed of lemon-scented risotto. Each bite reflects the essence of the valley — fresh, bright, and deeply satisfying.

3. Solar dos Peixes – Fall for the Grilled Octopus

Solar dos Peixes celebrates the bounty of both river and ocean. Their signature grilled octopus with smoked paprika oil is simply unforgettable. Tender yet charred in all the right places, the octopus rests on creamy sweet potato mash, dusted with sea salt crystals. It's a plate that looks like an artwork and tastes like a seafaring dream.

4. O Lagar Velho – Experience the Duck Rice

In a stone building that once pressed olives centuries ago, O Lagar Velho crafts dishes that honor old-world techniques. The house specialty, arroz de pato (duck rice), bursts with comforting flavors. Sliced duck breast nestles into seasoned rice, with hints of smoky chouriço and caramelized onions infusing every spoonful. Topped with a delicate scattering of crispy skin, it's rustic luxury on a plate.

5. Vinha Velha – Relish the Bacalhau à Brás

At Vinha Velha, where ancient vines coil around the terrace, you'll discover one of the finest versions of Bacalhau à Brás — Portugal's beloved cod dish. Salted cod is shredded and folded into silken scrambled eggs, fine matchstick potatoes, and a handful of fresh herbs. Bright and golden, the plate captures the Douro sun itself.

6. Encosta Dourada – Indulge in Smoked Pork Tenderloin

Tucked against golden hillsides, Encosta Dourada specializes in meats kissed by smoke and flame. Their must-try dish, the smoked pork tenderloin with fig reduction, balances the rich, savory meat with the gentle sweetness of ripe Douro figs. The result? A mouthwatering contrast that lingers long after your last bite.

7. Tasca do Vale – Celebrate the Rustic Stew

For a hearty and authentic meal, Tasca do Vale is an unbeatable choice. Their signature cozido à portuguesa

— a robust, slow-simmered stew of meats, sausages, and vegetables — arrives steaming and fragrant. Each forkful tells a story of the valley's farmers and traditions, where nothing goes to waste and everything is made with care.

8. Restaurante Rio Verde – Taste the River Shrimp Risotto

Perched at the water's edge, Restaurante Rio Verde brings a breezy freshness to its dishes. The crown jewel of the menu is the river shrimp risotto, creamy and brimming with the briny sweetness of freshwater shrimp. Finished with local herbs and a whisper of lemon zest, it's a celebration of river life on a plate.

9. Adega do Douro – Dive into the Roasted Lamb Shoulder

Inside an old wine cellar, Adega do Douro serves meals worthy of kings. Their roasted lamb shoulder, slow-cooked to fall-apart perfection, is seasoned simply with garlic, bay leaves, and Douro wine. The lamb is served alongside seasonal vegetables roasted in the same juices, creating a meal that's rich, earthy, and unforgettable.

10. Pedra do Rio – Feast on Wild Boar Ragout

Pedra do Rio captures the wilder side of the valley with its signature wild boar ragout. Simmered for hours in a hearty red wine reduction, the boar becomes meltingly tender. The ragout is spooned over hand-cut tagliatelle, offering a robust dish full of character and soul.

11. Azenha Real – Indulge in the Vineyard Chicken

In a converted 17th-century mill, Azenha Real offers a dish that pays homage to the surrounding vineyards: vineyard chicken. Marinated in young wine and slow-roasted with cloves, onions, and fresh herbs, the chicken emerges juicy and aromatic. Served with buttery crushed potatoes, this dish feels like a warm embrace from the land itself.

12. Cais da Memória – Marvel at the Port Wine Beef

Right by the rippling river, Cais da Memória transforms local staples into refined treasures. Their highlight is the beef tenderloin glazed with aged port wine. Each bite blends the richness of beef with the sweetness and depth of the region's famous fortified wine, creating a silky, almost luxurious flavor profile.

13. Páteo do Douro – Devour the Seafood Cataplana

Páteo do Douro brings a taste of the coast inland with their seafood cataplana — a colorful medley of clams, prawns, fish, and mussels simmered in a copper vessel with tomatoes, garlic, and white wine. It arrives bubbling and aromatic, inviting you to dive in and savor the flavors of Portugal's oceans and rivers.

14. Taberna da Quinta – Fall for the Veal Medallions

In an intimate setting surrounded by vines, Taberna da Quinta shines with its veal medallions in green peppercorn sauce. Perfectly seared and bathed in a rich yet slightly piquant sauce, the veal remains tender and succulent. Paired with a glass of local Touriga Nacional, it's a match made in heaven.

Chapter 7

Local Crafts and Souvenirs in Douro Valley for Tourists

The Douro Valley, with its winding riverbanks, terraced vineyards, and sun-drenched hills, is a treasure chest for visitors seeking more than just unforgettable views. Beyond its famed wines, this enchanting region offers a vibrant selection of local crafts and souvenirs — each telling a story of tradition, artistry, and pride.

Whether you're looking to bring home a piece of the valley or gift a slice of Portugal to someone special, here's a guide to the must-have items you'll find in Douro's charming towns and villages.

1. Hand-Painted Azulejos (Ceramic Tiles)

One of the most iconic and colorful souvenirs you can find in the Douro Valley is the hand-painted azulejo. These intricate ceramic tiles, often in blue-and-white designs or vivid multicolored scenes, have been a cornerstone of Portuguese artistry for centuries. In the Douro, artisans often depict rural life, vineyard scenes, and river landscapes unique to the region. These tiles can be purchased individually or assembled into panels — perfect for adorning a wall back home or using as decorative trivets and coasters.

2. Artisan Cork Products

Portugal is the world's leading producer of cork, and the Douro Valley certainly upholds this reputation with creative flair. Local craftsmen transform cork into an impressive array of items: handbags, wallets, hats, belts, shoes, and even jewelry. Not only are these products lightweight and eco-friendly, but they also carry a stylish rustic charm. A cork bag or set of cork coasters from the Douro is a trendy, sustainable souvenir that whispers authenticity.

3. Embroidered Linens and Lace

Another gem from the Douro Valley is its exquisite hand-embroidered linens. Tablecloths, napkins, handkerchiefs, and bed linens are meticulously stitched by local women, a skill passed down through generations. Delicate lacework borders many of these textiles, featuring traditional motifs such as grapevines, olive branches, and floral designs. Owning a piece of embroidered linen from the Douro feels like carrying home a fragment of its soul.

4. Traditional Pottery and Earthenware

In the quieter corners of the valley, you'll stumble upon workshops where potters craft charming earthenware using time-honored techniques. Rustic jugs, clay wine cups, olive bowls, and decorative plates are staples. Many pieces are hand-thrown and painted in earthy tones — terracotta, ochre, and deep green — colors that echo the valley's natural palette. These pottery items are functional and evoke the warmth of a traditional Portuguese kitchen.

5. Douro Wines and Port

It would be impossible to discuss souvenirs from the Douro without mentioning its world-famous wines. Vineyards cascade down the hillsides, producing not only celebrated Ports but also exceptional red and white wines. Tourists often love visiting quintas (wine estates) to sample and purchase bottles directly from the source. A carefully selected vintage, perhaps even with a personalized label from a boutique winery, makes for a sophisticated gift or keepsake that holds the taste of Douro in every sip.

6. Olive Oil and Gourmet Delicacies

Beyond the vineyards, olive groves flourish in the Douro Valley. The region's artisanal extra virgin olive oils are rich, fruity, and aromatic, often bottled attractively for tourists. Many shops also offer traditional food products like fig compotes, almonds roasted in honey, handmade jams, and preserved sausages. A gourmet basket from the Douro is a delicious reminder of the region's bounty.

7. Handmade Wooden Toys

In small villages sprinkled across the valley, you'll find workshops where skilled artisans create delightful hand-carved wooden toys. These toys — ranging from pull-along animals to colorful spinning tops — capture the simplicity and joy of traditional childhood. Each toy is lovingly crafted, sanded smooth, and sometimes hand-painted with vibrant colors. They make enchanting gifts, especially for young travelers or nostalgic adults.

8. Regional Jewelry

The jewelry crafted in the Douro region often draws inspiration from nature and local traditions. Filigree jewelry, in particular, is a standout. Delicate strands of gold or silver are twisted into intricate designs resembling flowers, hearts, and leaves. Some pieces incorporate motifs from Douro's river and vine culture. Whether it's a pair of earrings, a pendant, or a finely wrought bracelet, these handcrafted items bring a touch of elegance to any outfit.

9. Embroidered Festival Costumes (Miniature Versions)

While full traditional costumes may be too bulky to take home, many shops sell miniature versions of embroidered festival outfits. These detailed pieces represent the colorful garments worn during local celebrations. They often include miniature embroidered aprons, velvet waistcoats, and lace-trimmed skirts. Displayed in shadow boxes or frames, they make charming souvenirs capturing the spirit of Douro festivities.

10. Local Artworks and Paintings

The dramatic scenery of the Douro Valley has long inspired painters and sketch artists. In galleries and street markets, tourists can find original artworks — from watercolor landscapes to bold acrylics depicting vineyard scenes, river views, and traditional rabelo boats. A small painting or print rolled carefully into your suitcase becomes not just a souvenir, but a window back into your Douro experience whenever you glance at it.

11. Basketry and Woven Goods

Basket weaving remains a cherished tradition in the rural pockets of Douro. Using willow, straw, and cane, artisans fashion handmade baskets in various sizes and shapes. Some are designed for gathering grapes during harvest, while others are woven into stylish handbags and home decor. These durable, beautiful pieces offer a rustic yet elegant nod to Douro's agricultural heart.

12. Honey and Bee Products

Beekeeping thrives in the wild, floral stretches of the Douro Valley. Tourists will often find artisanal honey, beeswax candles, and even propolis tinctures sold at local markets. The honey, ranging from light and floral to dark and robust, captures the flavors of wild lavender, rosemary, and orange blossom. A jar of Douro honey is like bottling a little bit of the valley's sunshine.

13. Scented Soaps and Natural Cosmetics

Boutiques throughout the Douro Valley offer natural soaps and cosmetics made with local ingredients such as olive oil, grape extracts, and almond milk. These products are often crafted in small batches, wrapped in elegant packaging that reflects the valley's organic beauty. A bar of fragrant soap or a bottle of moisturizing oil offers a touch of Douro indulgence long after your journey ends.

14. Handcrafted Musical Instruments

In some traditional villages, musicians and artisans collaborate to craft regional musical instruments like cavaquinhos (small string instruments), tambourines, and Portuguese guitars. Though full-sized guitars may be a challenge to carry, smaller instruments or miniature versions make meaningful souvenirs, especially for music lovers enchanted by Portugal's soulful melodies.

Popular Shopping Centers in Douro Valley

1. Peso da Régua Riverside Market

In the beating heart of Peso da Régua, this market is a colorful fusion of culture, flavor, and craftsmanship. Every weekend, local vendors set up their wooden stalls along the Douro's banks, creating an irresistible scene for shoppers and wanderers alike. Here, visitors can sift through locally made ceramics, rustic textiles, handwoven baskets, and, of course, a bounty of wine-related goods. The riverside breeze, lively chatter in Portuguese, and smell of fresh pastries from nearby cafés make every shopping trip here feel like a slice of authentic life.

2. Vila Real Shopping Center

Vila Real, often called the "capital" of the Douro region, boasts one of the few formal shopping complexes within driving distance — the Vila Real Shopping Center. It isn't an overwhelmingly large mall, but it is packed with popular Portuguese and European brands. Fashion boutiques, tech shops, and stylish home décor stores sit alongside cozy cafés. After a day wandering through vineyards and palaces, visitors often appreciate the convenience of this spot, where they can find both practical essentials and stylish souvenirs under one roof.

3. Lamego Artisan Square

Lamego, a historic town famed for its baroque sanctuary and elegant avenues, offers a charming artisan square that feels like stepping back in time. This small yet lively gathering place is dotted with stalls and tiny shops where craftsmen and women proudly display their goods. Think embroidered linens, delicate lacework, intricate azulejos (painted tiles), and rich leather products. Many shops offer personalized items, making this a dream location for travelers who want to take home a truly unique piece of the Douro.

4. Douro Wine Shops and Boutiques

Throughout the valley, wine boutiques are a kind of shopping center unto themselves. Nearly every vineyard offers a well-curated shop where visitors can purchase bottles unavailable anywhere else in the world. Beyond wine, these boutiques often sell olive oils, honey, almonds, and gourmet jams, each infused with the flavors of the Douro. Some favorites include the wine shops attached to quintas (wine estates), where tasting the goods before buying them is all part of the irresistible charm.

5. Mercado Municipal de Vila Real

This historic market is where locals go about their daily shopping, and where travelers looking for authenticity will feel right at home. The Mercado Municipal de Vila Real isn't glossy or touristy — it's vibrant, noisy, and full of life. From glistening stacks of fresh fish to fragrant bundles of herbs and handmade cheeses, the market offers a deep dive into the valley's culinary culture. Upstairs, visitors often find stands selling kitchenware, clothes, and traditional woven goods, ideal for those hunting for practical souvenirs with soul.

6. Peso da Régua Wine and Craft Stores

In Peso da Régua's narrow streets, several independent shops specialize in everything Douro. Inside these stores, rustic wooden shelves bow under the weight of port, table wines, and spirits. But wine isn't the only star. You'll discover hand-painted tiles, cork accessories (wallets, purses, jewelry), local embroidery, and even gourmet salt from the nearby Portuguese coast. Shop owners here are friendly, eager to explain the story behind every object, which transforms a simple purchase into a memory.

7. Pinhão Boutique Stalls

Pinhão is a postcard-perfect town where the river bends gracefully between emerald hills. Small boutique stalls scattered around the railway station and along the waterfront cater to visitors looking for something special. Embellished cork products, artisanal soaps infused with port wine or lavender, and watercolors painted by local artists are among the most sought-after items. Many vendors here are artists themselves, and chatting with them often reveals fascinating insights into Douro life and traditions.

8. Artisan Craft Fairs in Douro Villages

Many of the Douro's villages, such as São João da Pesqueira and Tabuaço, host regular artisan fairs, particularly during festivals and special weekends. These gatherings overflow with stalls where craftsmen showcase everything from hand-carved olive wood utensils to intricate gold filigree jewelry. Unlike more commercial shopping experiences, these fairs encourage slow browsing, friendly conversations, and a deep appreciation for the time-honored techniques behind every creation.

9. Douro Museum Gift Shop

Tucked inside Peso da Régua's famed Douro Museum, the museum shop offers one of the region's best collections of Douro-themed souvenirs. Beyond the expected postcards and books, shoppers find high-quality artisanal pieces: jewelry inspired by river motifs, limited-edition wines, curated gourmet baskets, and beautifully illustrated guides. It's an ideal stop for those seeking meaningful gifts that tell the story of the valley's heritage and soul.

10. Lamego's Saturday Farmer's Market

Every Saturday, Lamego's main square comes alive with a farmer's market that's as much about shopping as it is about community. Besides the abundance of fresh produce, visitors find stalls filled with jams, cheeses, sweets, olive oils, and baked goods, each carrying the unmistakable taste of the Douro soil. Artisans selling handcrafts, flowers, and colorful traditional dolls complete the scene, making it a sensory-rich shopping experience like no other.

11. Peso da Régua Antique Shops

Hidden along the backstreets of Peso da Régua are a handful of charming antique stores that collectors and curious shoppers adore. These places brim with treasures: vintage port wine bottles, hand-carved furniture, century-old books, and decorative tiles salvaged from ancient estates. Each piece here seems to whisper stories from Douro's layered past, making shopping an almost archaeological adventure.

12. Boutique Cork Shops

Portugal is the world's largest producer of cork, and in the Douro Valley, cork is celebrated as an art form. Boutique shops specializing in cork goods can be found throughout the region, particularly in towns like Lamego and Peso da Régua. These aren't your average cork boards — think chic handbags, eco-friendly shoes, stylish hats, and even cork umbrellas. Each item is durable, sustainable, and fashionable, reflecting Portugal's flair for blending tradition with innovation.

13. Regional Wine Cooperatives

Scattered throughout the valley are regional wine cooperatives where local growers band together to sell their harvests. These centers often include retail spaces that are perfect for stocking up on excellent wines at friendly prices. Visitors can chat with passionate growers, taste different varietals, and leave with cases of wine that often remain undiscovered by larger tourist crowds.

15. Pinhão Train Station Gift Store

The Pinhão train station is famous for its azulejo tile panels depicting scenes from Douro's wine culture. Attached to this heritage landmark is a small but fascinating gift shop where travelers can purchase replicas of the iconic tiles, art prints, regional wines, and hand-stitched goods. It's an unmissable stop for anyone who appreciates history, craftsmanship, and the poetic beauty of the Douro Valley.

Chapter 8

Nightlife Activities for Tourists to Explore in Douro Valley

The Douro Valley may be celebrated for its sun-drenched vineyards and serene river views by day, but as the sun dips behind the rolling hills, a different kind of magic awakens. Evenings here are woven with rich culture, mellow entertainment, and subtle surprises. For travelers wondering what to do once twilight descends, the Douro Valley offers a range of enchanting nighttime activities that blend relaxation, local flavor, and vibrant ambiance. Here are some unforgettable ways to enjoy the Douro after dark.

1. Wine Tasting Under the Stars

One cannot talk about the Douro Valley without mentioning wine. Several quintas (wine estates) offer nighttime wine tastings, an experience that feels especially magical beneath a sky dusted with stars. Picture yourself swirling a glass of velvety Port or crisp Douro white while surrounded by ancient vineyards bathed in moonlight. Some estates even pair the tastings with candlelit dinners, live fado music, or private vineyard tours, making the night feel utterly timeless.

2. Riverfront Dining with Live Music

The towns of Peso da Régua, Pinhão, and Lamego boast charming riverfront restaurants that come alive at night. Soft melodies from local musicians often spill out onto the cobblestone streets, blending with the gentle ripple of the Douro River. Whether it's a jazz trio, acoustic guitarists, or a lively folk band, the experience of savoring fresh grilled fish, regional meats, and robust wines while immersed in soulful tunes creates an unforgettable evening.

3. Sunset Cruises on the Douro River

While daytime cruises along the Douro River are popular, an evening or sunset cruise holds a special kind of romance. Some operators offer twilight sailings where guests can enjoy a glass of Port while drifting past illuminated vineyards, centuries-old villages, and rugged hillsides that glow in the fading light. The calm waters reflect the colors of the sunset, creating a serene, almost dreamlike atmosphere that lingers long after the cruise ends.

4. Strolling through Historic Town Centers

Douro Valley Travel Guide 2025

Places like Peso da Régua, Vila Real, and Pinhão transform at night into hushed, atmospheric villages where history whispers from stone walls and tiled churches. Wandering the narrow, winding streets under vintage lamplight feels like stepping back in time. Hidden courtyards, quiet chapels, and quaint squares reveal themselves as you meander, perhaps stopping for a late-night espresso or a slice of local almond cake at a tucked-away café.

5. Fado Evenings in Traditional Taverns

Fado, the soulful music of Portugal, captures the heart of the Douro after dark. Some intimate taverns and wine bars host live fado performances where the heartfelt vocals and melancholic guitar melodies tell stories of love, longing, and nostalgia. Listening to fado in a small, candlelit room with a glass of aged Port in hand is an emotional experience — one that feels deeply authentic to the spirit of the Douro Valley.

6. Attend a Local Festival or Festa

Throughout the year, Douro Valley villages host vibrant festivals that often stretch late into the night. From wine harvest celebrations in autumn to Saint John festivities in June, these lively events offer music, dancing, fireworks, and plenty of local delicacies. Tourists are always welcome, and it's a brilliant opportunity to mingle with locals, sample rustic dishes like roasted sardines or suckling pig, and join in folk dances that have been passed down through generations.

7. Night Photography Tours

For shutterbugs and amateur photographers, the Douro Valley's nighttime vistas offer endless inspiration. Some local guides organize night photography tours, helping visitors capture the twinkling lights of river towns, starlit vineyards, and ancient bridges reflected in dark waters. Even casual photographers will find it hard to resist snapping the silhouetted hillsides against a shimmering sky.

8. Wine Cellar Tours by Lantern Light

Certain historic wine cellars offer nocturnal tours by lantern light, adding a dash of mystery to the already atmospheric underground spaces. Walking among the oak barrels, breathing in the rich scents of aging wine, and learning about centuries-old techniques feels almost sacred at night. Some tours finish with tastings of rare vintages rarely poured during daytime visits, making the experience even more special.

Douro Valley Travel Guide 2025

9. Spa Evenings at Luxury Wine Hotels

After a long day of vineyard hopping or hiking, an evening spa session can be pure bliss. Many upscale wine hotels and quintas have luxurious spas offering nighttime treatments — think grape-seed oil massages, vinotherapy facials, or aromatic steam baths infused with local herbs. Some spas even have outdoor pools where you can float under the stars, glass of wine in hand, as the countryside hums softly around you.

10. Cooking Classes and Gastronomic Experiences

Nighttime is also when many culinary schools and boutique hotels host cooking classes centered on traditional Douro Valley recipes. Tourists can learn to prepare regional dishes like bacalhau à brás (salt cod with potatoes and eggs) or cozido à portuguesa (hearty meat stew), guided by passionate local chefs. After the hands-on session, everyone sits down together to savor their creations, often paired with the perfect Douro wine, turning the evening into both an education and a celebration.

11. Open-Air Cinema Nights

During summer months, some vineyards and towns organize open-air movie nights where locals and visitors alike gather under the stars to watch classic films or Portuguese cinema. Blankets, wine, and shared laughter fill the night air. These casual gatherings capture the simple, communal spirit that defines the Douro Valley, offering a relaxed and memorable way to wind down an evening.

12. Bar-Hopping in Peso da Régua

For those seeking a livelier night out, Peso da Régua offers a modest yet charming bar scene. From chic wine bars with panoramic terraces to cozy pubs serving craft beer and cocktails, there's a delightful variety of places to hop between. Unlike the raucous nightlife of big cities, the bars here maintain a friendly, laid-back vibe where locals and tourists mingle easily, stories are exchanged, and friendships are often sparked over shared bottles of wine.

13. Moonlit Walks along the Douro River

Few experiences are as soothing as a leisurely, moonlit walk along the Douro River. The water sparkles under the night sky, boats gently bob along their moorings, and the cool night air carries the faint scent of grapes and wildflowers. It's the perfect way to reflect on the day's adventures, enjoy quiet conversation, or simply absorb the valley's timeless beauty at your own pace.

14. Visit a Wine Lounge or Tasting Room

Several quintas and boutique hotels now offer chic wine lounges where you can sample flights of Douro wines in a stylish, relaxed setting. With comfy seating, low lighting, and knowledgeable staff, these spaces are ideal for those who prefer a refined, intimate evening activity. Some lounges offer food pairings like artisan cheeses, olives, or delicate pastries, elevating the tasting experience into a full sensory journey.

7 Days Itinerary Plans for Tourists in Douro Valley

Day 1: Arrival and Porto Exploration

Start your Douro adventure in Porto, the gateway to the valley. After arriving, allow yourself a day to settle in and soak up the character of this lively riverside city. Stroll along the historic Ribeira District, admire the colorful facades, and sip a glass of port wine by the water. Cross the Dom Luís I Bridge for a breathtaking view of the Douro River shimmering below.

In the evening, treat yourself to a cozy dinner at a riverside restaurant. Porto's atmosphere is the perfect overture for the wonders waiting upriver.

Day 2: Scenic Train Journey to Peso da Régua

Begin your day with a scenic train ride from Porto's São Bento Station to Peso da Régua. The journey itself feels like a moving postcard, gliding past emerald hills, quaint villages, and steep vineyards carved into the valley walls.

Once in Régua, visit the Douro Museum to get a rich overview of the region's winemaking heritage and cultural traditions. Later, walk through the town's charming streets or relax along the riverbank, where traditional rabelo boats bob gently on the water. Spend the night in a local guesthouse to truly immerse yourself in the valley's gentle rhythm.

Day 3: Vineyard Tours and Wine Tasting

No trip to Douro Valley would be complete without exploring its legendary vineyards. Dedicate today to visiting quintas (wine estates), where generations have perfected the art of crafting exquisite wines.

Book a guided tour at Quinta do Vallado or Quinta da Pacheca, where you can wander through sun-kissed vineyards, learn the secrets of wine production, and, of course, indulge in tastings of both rich port and elegant table wines. Pair the tastings with regional delicacies like cured meats, cheeses, and olive oil, all while basking in sweeping valley views.

Day 4: River Cruise and Pinhão Discovery

Today offers a slower, almost meditative pace. Embark on a river cruise from Peso da Régua to Pinhão, often hailed as the heart of the Douro. The slow-moving boat ride offers a dreamlike perspective of terraced slopes and tiny villages hugging the river's edge.

Upon arriving in Pinhão, visit the Pinhão Railway Station, famous for its intricate azulejo tiles depicting scenes from vineyard life. Afterward, wander through the town or take a short hike to a nearby viewpoint for panoramic vistas. End the day with a sunset dinner overlooking the river, savoring the gentle hum of countryside life.

Day 5: Hidden Villages and Olive Oil Tastings

While wine dominates the Douro's fame, the region's olive oil deserves its own standing ovation. Drive or join a tour towards the Alijó and Favaios areas, where centuries-old olive groves and traditional villages invite exploration.

Visit a working olive estate to see how golden, aromatic olive oil is crafted, and taste fresh, peppery oils paired with rustic bread. In Favaios, sample the town's famed fortified wine, Moscatel de Favaios, and linger in its sleepy squares where time seems to have slowed down decades ago.

Day 6: Hiking Trails and Viewpoints

Today is for the active soul. Lace up your hiking boots and explore one of the valley's many trails that weave through vineyards, forests, and hillsides.

The São Leonardo de Galafura viewpoint is a must-visit — often described as offering the most soul-stirring panorama of the Douro Valley. If you prefer a more structured path, the PR1 Caminho do Viinho trail near Provesende winds through terraced vineyards and ancient estates, offering a real connection to the land. Pack a picnic to enjoy amid the vines, surrounded by nothing but bird song and the whisper of the wind.

Day 7: Relaxation and Farewell in Lamego

Conclude your Douro odyssey in the graceful town of Lamego, a place where history and tranquility blend seamlessly. Climb the ornate baroque staircase leading to the Sanctuary of Our Lady of Remedies, or meander through cobblestone streets lined with Renaissance fountains and charming shops.

Treat yourself to a leisurely lunch featuring local specialties like bola de Lamego (a savory bread stuffed with smoked meats) paired with a crisp white wine. Before leaving, take a moment at one of the quiet viewpoints to reflect on the week's experiences — the flavors, the vistas, the warmth of the Douro's embrace.

Printed in Dunstable, United Kingdom

Printed in Great Britain
by Amazon